HANDBOOK OF VOCABULARY TEACHING STRATEGIES
Communication Activities with the *Word by Word Picture Dictionary*

Steven J. Molinsky
Bill Bliss

Contributing Author: Diane Terry

PRENTICE HALL REGENTS
Upper Saddle River, New Jersey 07458

Library of Congress Cataloging-in-Publication Data

Molinsky, Steven J.
    Handbook of vocabulary teaching strategies: communication activities with the word
by word picture dictionary / Steven J. Molinsky, Bill Bliss; contributing author, Diane Terry.
        p.   cm.
    Includes index.
    ISBN 01-3-278441-6
    1. English language—Study and teaching—Foreign speakers—Aids and devices.
2. Vocabulary—Study and teaching—Aids and devices. 3. Vocabulary—Problems, exercises, etc.
4. Activity programs in education.   I. Bliss, Bill.   II. Title.
PE1128.A2M557   1994
428.1'07—dc20   93–49401 CIP

Publisher: *Tina Carver*
Director of Production and Manufacturing: *David Riccardi*
Electronic Production Coordinator: *Molly Pike Riccardi*
Creative Director: *Paula Maylahn*

Editorial Production / Design Manager: *Dominick Mosco*
Production supervision: *Paula D. Williams*
Electronic production and interior page design: *D. Andrew Gitzy*
Cover Design Coordinator: *Merle Krumper*
Cover Design: *Paul Belfanti*
Production Coordinator: *Ray Keating*

 © 1994 by Prentice Hall Regents
Prentice-Hall, Inc.
Simon & Schuster / A Viacom Company
Upper Saddle River, New Jersey 07458

Printed in the United States of America

10   9   8   7   6

ISBN 0-13-278441-6

Prentice Hall International (UK) Limited, *London*
Prentice Hall of Australia Pty. Limited, *Sydney*
Prentice Hall Canada, Inc., *Toronto*
Prentice Hall Hispanoamericana, S.A., *Mexico*
Prentice Hall Of India Private Limited, *New Delhi*
Prentice Hall of Japan, Inc., *Tokyo*
Simon & Schuster Asia Pte. Ltd., *Singapore*
Editora Prentice Hall do Brasil, Ltda., *Rio de Janeiro*

CONTENTS

J. DISCUSSION

K. RESEARCH

L. EXTENSIONS

INTRODUCTION

This handbook is designed to serve as a basic guide to communicative strategies for vocabulary development. Over 75 interactive, student-centered activities are presented, with examples based on the *Word by Word Picture Dictionary*. In addition, a brief summary of approaches for introducing and practicing the vocabulary in *Word by Word* is presented.

This handbook is appropriate both as a companion manual for users of *Word by Word*, as well as a professional reference tool for new teachers, experienced teachers, and teachers-in-training.

THE *WORD BY WORD* PICTURE DICTIONARY

The *Word by Word Picture Dictionary* presents more than 3000 vocabulary words in over 100 thematic units that range from the immediate world of the student to the world at large. The vocabulary is depicted in detailed illustrations containing numbered cues that are correlated to a list of the words below. The illustrations are also available as wall charts and overhead transparencies.

Word by Word provides model conversations that enable students to engage in interactive conversational practice with the vocabulary words. In addition, writing and discussion questions in every unit encourage students to share experiences, thoughts, opinions, and information about themselves, their cultures, and their countries.

TEACHING STRATEGIES

The *Word by Word Teacher's Resource Book* is a complete, comprehensive source of language and culture notes related to the *Word by Word Picture Dictionary* vocabulary as well as suggested teaching strategies for introducing and practicing the words in each unit. The following is a summary of these approaches and strategies— all designed to actively involve students in their acquisition of English vocabulary.

1. *Previewing the Vocabulary:* Activate students' prior knowledge of the vocabulary by either brainstorming with students the words in the unit they already know and writing them on the board, or by having students look at the Wall Chart, the transparency, or the illustration in *Word by Word* and identifying the words they are familiar with.

2. Presenting the Vocabulary: Point to the picture of each word, say the word, and have the class repeat it chorally and individually. Check students' understanding and pronunciation of the vocabulary.

3. *Vocabulary Practice:* Have students practice the vocabulary as a class, in pairs, or in small groups. Say or write a word, and have students point to the item or tell the number. Or, point to an item or give the number, and have students say the word.

4. *Model Conversation Practice:* Some units have model conversations that use the first word in the vocabulary list. Other models are in the form of *skeletal dialogs*, in which vocabulary words can be inserted. (In many skeletal dialogs, bracketed numbers indicate which words can be used to practice the conversation. If no bracketed numbers appear, all the words on the page can be used.)

   The following steps are recommended for Model Conversation Practice:

   a. Preview. Students look at the model illustration and discuss who they think the speakers are and where the conversation takes place.

   b. The teacher presents the model and checks students' understanding of the situation and the vocabulary.

   c. Students repeat each line of the conversation chorally or individually.

   d. Students practice the model in pairs.

   e. A pair of students presents a new conversation based on the model, but using a different word from the vocabulary list.

   f. In pairs, students practice several new conversations based on the model, using different vocabulary words.

   g. Pairs present their conversations to the class.

5. *Additional Conversation Practice:* Many units provide two additional skeletal dialogs for further conversation practice with the vocabulary. (These can be found in a yellow-shaded area at the bottom of the page.) Have students practice and present these conversations using any words they wish.

6. *Writing and Spelling Practice:* Have students practice spelling the words as a class, in pairs, or in small groups. Say or spell a word, and have students write it and then point to the picture of the item or tell the number. Or, point to a picture of an item or give the number, and have students write the word.

7. *Themes for Discussion, Composition, Journals, and Portfolios:* Each unit of *Word by Word* provides one or more questions for discussion and composition. (These can be found in a green-shaded area at the bottom of the page.) Have students respond to the questions as a class, in pairs, or in small groups. Or, have students write their responses at home, share their written work with other students, and discuss as a class, in pairs, or in small groups.

Students may enjoy keeping a journal of their written work. If time permits, you may want to write a response in each student's journal, sharing your opinions and experiences as well as reacting to what the student has written. If you are keeping portfolios of students' work, these compositions serve as excellent samples of students' progress in learning English.

COMMUNICATION ACTIVITIES

Each unit of the *Word by Word Teacher's Resource Book* provides a wealth of games, tasks, brainstorming, discussion, movement, drawing, miming, role-playing and other activities designed to take advantage of students' different learning styles and particular abilities and strengths. These activities can be categorized based on the type of task involved:

A. **Naming**—activities based on *saying* vocabulary words.

B. **Identifying**—activities based on identifying words from pictures or actions.

C. **Definitions**—activities based on defining words.

D. **Clues**—activities in which clues to the meanings of words are given.

E. **Asking Questions**—activities in which students ask questions related to the words.

F. **Categories**—activities in which students categorize words according to their meanings.

G. **Associations**—activities based on brainstorming associations with the vocabulary words.

H. **Connections**—activities focusing on the relationships between vocabulary words.

I. **Dialogs**—activities in which the words are practiced conversationally.

J. **Discussion**—activities based on talking about the words.

K. **Research**—activities based on finding out further information about the vocabulary words.

L. **Extensions**—activities based on using the vocabulary words in additional contexts.

The following is a summary of 77 of these activities—a brief description of each activity with an example from a particular unit of the Picture Dictionary. We encourage you to adapt these activities to whatever group of words you wish. Our goal is to enable you to provide your students with an enjoyable and interactive way of practicing the vocabulary *word by word.*

NAMING

1. BEANBAG TOSS

Students call out vocabulary items while tossing a beanbag to each other.

Sample Activity for Word by Word Picture Dictionary pages 4–5:
North America

Have students toss a beanbag back and forth. The student to whom the beanbag is tossed must name a place in North America.

2. CHAIN GAME

Students extend a sentence by adding more and more vocabulary items.

Sample Activity for Word by Word Picture Dictionary page 65:
The Toy Store

a. Begin by saying, "I went to the toy store and bought a jump rope."

b. Student 1 repeats what you said and adds another item. For example, "I went to the toy store and bought a jump rope and construction paper."

c. Have successive students continue repeating everything the previous students said while adding another toy store item.

3. CLAP IN RHYTHM

Students call out vocabulary items while clapping their hands.

Sample Activity for Word by Word Picture Dictionary pages 92–93:
The Car

Object: Once a clapping rhythm is established, the students must continue naming different *car words.*

a. Have students sit in a circle.

b. Establish a steady even beat: one-two-three-four, one-two-three-four, etc. by having students clap their hands to their laps twice and then clap their hands together twice. Repeat throughout the game, maintaining the same rhythm.

c. The object is for each student in turn to name a car word *each time the hands are clapped together twice.* Nothing is said when students clap their hands on their laps.

Note: The beat never stops! If a student misses a beat, he or she can either wait for the next beat or else pass to the next student.

4. LETTER GAME

Students name vocabulary items starting with different letters.

Sample Activity for Word by Word Picture Dictionary page 45:
Vegetables

a. Divide the class into two teams.

b. Say, "I'm thinking of a vegetable that starts with *a.*"

c. The first person to raise his or her hand and guess correctly (*asparagus*) wins a point for that team.

d. Continue with other letters of the alphabet.

The team that gets the most correct answers wins the game.

5. LINKING WORDS

Students link words to each other through common shared letters.

Sample Activity for Word by Word Picture Dictionary page 75:
The Post Office

   a. Print one of the vocabulary words on page 75 of the Picture Dictionary in the upper left corner of the board.

   b. Have the first student think of another related word that begins with the last letter of the word on the board and *link* that word onto the word on the board in *stair* fashion.

   c. Proceed this way with each student linking a word onto the end of the previous word. For example:

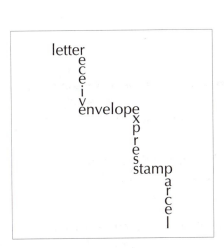

6. COMICAL PHRASES

Students create comical phrases with adjectives plus the vocabulary items.

Sample Activity for Word by Word Picture Dictionary page 44:
Fruits

FUNNY FRUITS!

Have students associate the name of a fruit with an adjective having the same initial letter. For example:

> an _a_wful _a_pple
> a _b_ad _b_anana
> a _m_ixed-up _m_ango

Have students draw pictures of their *funny fruits*.

7. STAND IN LINE

Students arrange themselves in a line based on the vocabulary items.

Sample Activity for Word by Word Picture Dictionary page 33:
The Calendar

VARIATION 1: Write each month of the year on a separate card and distribute randomly to students. Have them line themselves up chronologically starting from January.

VARIATION 2: Have students arrange themselves in a line according to their birth dates (month and day only). They will need to ask and answer questions in order to line themselves up chronologically from the date closest to January 1st through the date closest to December 31st.

VARIATION 3: Have students arrange themselves in a line according to some important date in their lives (month, day, and year), such as the date they began to study English or moved to their present home.

8. TELEPHONE

Students take turns whispering a phrase containing a vocabulary word.

Sample Activity for Word by Word Picture Dictionary page 74:
Medicine

    a. Have students sit in a circle or semi-circle.

    b. Whisper some instructions for taking medication to the first student.
       For example:

               "Take two tablets every four hours with food."

    c. The first student whispers what he or she heard to the second student, and so forth around the room. When the *message* gets to the last student, that person says it aloud. Is it the message you started with?

    d. Give each student in the class a chance to start his or her own telephone message.

IDENTIFYING

9. DESCRIBING PICTURES

Students describe pictures containing vocabulary items.

Sample Activity for Word by Word Picture Dictionary page 57:
Clothing

Bring in pictures from magazines, newspapers, or mail order clothing catalogs that depict items presented in this unit. As a class, in pairs, or in small groups, have students describe what the people in the pictures are wearing.

10. DRAWING GAME

Students draw vocabulary items for others to guess.

Sample Activity for Word by Word Picture Dictionary page 60:
Jewelry and Accessories

You will need either an hourglass or a watch with a second hand on it for timing this game.

Make up identical sets of cards with the names of jewelry and accessories written on them and have two piles on a table or desk in the front of the room. Also, place a pad of paper and pencil next to each team's set of cards.

a. Divide the class into two teams. Have each team sit together in a different part of the room.

b. When you say, "Go!", a person from each team comes to the front of his or her team, picks a card from the pile, and draws the object. The rest of the team then guesses what the object is.

c. When a team correctly guesses an object, another team member picks a card and draws the object written on that card.

d. Continue until each team has guessed all of the objects in their pile.

The team that guesses the objects in the shortest time wins the game.

11. PICTURE THIS!

Students draw what you describe.

Sample Activity for Word by Word Picture Dictionary page 14:
The Living Room

Describe a living room and have students draw what you describe. You can either *invent* a living room or describe a picture you have taken from a magazine. For example:

> "In this living room, there's a fireplace on the left wall. In front of the fireplace there are two loveseats, one on either side of the fireplace. Over the fireplace, . . . "

VARIATION 1: Do the above activity in pairs, where students take turns describing different living rooms for the other to draw.

VARIATION 2: One student comes to the board and the rest of the class gives instructions for that student to draw a living room on the board.

12. READ, WRITE, AND DRAW

Students write each other letters using the vocabulary items.

Sample Activity for Word by Word Picture Dictionary page 17:
The Bedroom

Students write each other letters in which they describe their bedrooms. Students exchange letters and draw pictures to illustrate what they read in the letters.

13. FLASH CARDS

Students identify pictures of vocabulary items.

Sample Activity for Word by Word Picture Dictionary pages 50–51:
Containers and Quantities

Bring in pictures of supermarket items. Have students identify the items as you hold up the pictures. For example: *a jar of mayonnaise, two bags of cookies, a head of cabbage.* This activity can also be done in pairs or in small groups.

14. GRAB BAG

Students try to guess items hidden in paper bags.

Sample Activity for Word by Word Picture Dictionary page 89:
Office Supplies

WHAT'S IN THE BAG? [VARIATION 1]

Collect as many small office supplies as there are students in the class and put the items in a large bag. Have each student put his or her hand in the bag, feel an object, and try to guess what it is.

WHAT'S IN THE BAG? [VARIATION 2]

a. Collect a variety of small office supplies and put each one in a small brown lunch-size bag. Put all the bags on a desk or table in front of the room.

b. Divide the class into pairs. One member of the pair goes to the desk, takes a bag, and looks inside.

c. The second partner tries to guess what is in the bag by asking questions.

d. When the second partner has guessed the object, he or she returns the bag to the desk and gets another one for the first partner to guess.

15. LISTEN AND NUMBER

Students make up stories using the vocabulary items and listen for key vocabulary items.

Sample Activity for Word by Word Picture Dictionary page 9:
Everyday Activities II

a. Divide the class into pairs.

b. Partner A and Partner B should both look at the pictures on page 9 of the Picture Dictionary.

c. Partner A chooses 6 of the activities depicted and makes up a story about them.

d. Partner B listens to the story and numbers the pictures in the order he or she hears them in Partner A's story.

e. Reverse roles.

16. LOCATIONS

Students identify vocabulary items based on their location in the illustration in the Picture Dictionary.

Sample Activity for Word by Word Picture Dictionary pages 38–39:
The City

Have students look at the Wall Chart, the transparency, or the illustration on pages 38–39 of the Picture Dictionary and answer questions about the location of people and places in the city. For example:

> A. Where's the jail?
> B. It's behind the police station.
>
> A. Where's the ice cream truck?
> B. It's on the corner, next to the courthouse.

VARIATION 1: Do the activity in pairs or small groups, with students asking as well as answering the questions.

VARIATION 2: Do the activity as a listening exercise, in which you give the location and students tell what you're describing. For example:

> A. It's on the street in front of the bus.
> B. The taxi.
>
> A. It's near the corner, on the sidewalk, next to the fire station.
> B. The phone booth.

VARIATION 3: Do this activity in pairs or small groups, with students taking turns telling the locations.

VARIATION 4: Divide the class into teams and do all of these activities as games.

17. TALK IN CIRCLES

> Students tell the locations of vocabulary items from the Picture Dictionary in a *circular* fashion.

Sample Activity for Word by Word Picture Dictionary page 29:
Gardening Tools and Home Supplies

a. Write on the board:

next to	behind	above
between	in front of	below

b. Have students take turns asking and answering questions about the location of different objects on page 29 of the Picture Dictionary. For example:

Student 1: Where's the shovel?
Student 2: Next to the hedge clippers.
　　　　　 [to Student 3]
　　　　　 Where are the hedge clippers?
Student 3: Above the wheelbarrow.
　　　　　 [to Student 4]
　　　　　 Where's the wheelbarrow?

18. MIME

> Students pantomime vocabulary items.

Sample Activity for Word by Word Picture Dictionary page 23:
Personal Care Products

a. Write words from page 23 of the Picture Dictionary on cards.

b. Have each student take a turn picking a card from the pile and pantomiming the object written on the card or what someone might do with the object.

c. Other students then guess what the object is.

VARIATION: Do the activity with two competing teams.

19. TPR

Students act out commands with the vocabulary items.

Sample Activity for Word by Word Picture Dictionary page 108:
Sport and Exercise Actions

SIMON SAYS

This game consists of a series of rapid commands which students follow only when the command is preceded by the words *Simon says.* If the student follows the command when the words *Simon says* are not spoken, that student must sit down. The last student to remain standing wins the game.

a. Have all the students stand up.

b. Say, "Simon says stretch." (The students stretch.)

c. Say, "Simon says bend." (The students bend.)

d. Say, "Hop!" (Any students who hop must sit down and not continue to play.)

Note: Say the commands in rapid order to allow as little time as possible to think about *Simon says.*

VARIATION: Have different students take turns leading the game.

20. PUZZLES

Students put together puzzles depicting vocabulary items.

Sample Activity for Word by Word Picture Dictionary page 18:
The Kitchen

    a. Cut out several pictures of kitchens from magazines. Paste each picture on a piece of cardboard or other heavy paper and cut the picture into four or more pieces.

    b. Give each student a piece from one of the puzzles and tell students to walk around the room and find other pieces to make a complete picture.

    The object is not to show each other the puzzle pieces, but to offer information and gather information from others. For example:

> "My picture has a yellow refrigerator on the left wall."
> "There's a round kitchen table with four chairs in my picture."
> "Is there a trash compactor in your kitchen?"

    c. Continue the activity until all the puzzle pieces are matched. The group that matches their puzzle first wins.

21. REALIA

Students bring in real world examples of vocabulary items.

Sample Activity for Word by Word Picture Dictionary page 64:
Computers, Telephones, and Cameras

COMPARISON SHOPPING

    a. Tell students to cut out advertisements for computers, telephones, and cameras from newspapers and magazines.

    b. As a class, in pairs, or in small groups, have students compare prices and features of the different products.

22. REMEMBERING

Students try to remember items in the illustration in the Picture Dictionary.

Sample Activity for Word by Word Picture Dictionary page 25:
Outside the Home

a. Tell students to spend 3 minutes looking very carefully at the front and back yards depicted on page 25 of the Picture Dictionary.

b. Have students close their books and write down what they remember about the scenes.

c. Have students compare notes with a partner and then look at the pictures in the Picture Dictionary to see how well they remembered the scenes.

VARIATION 1: Instead of students writing descriptions, ask them questions about the scenes to see how much they remember. For example:

> How many windows are there in the front of the house?
> Is the back door open?
> What's on the patio?

VARIATION 2: Have students do this activity in pairs, with partners taking turns asking and answering questions about the pictures.

VARIATION 3: Divide the class into several teams and do the activity as a game in which team members help each other to remember. The team with the most correct answers wins the game.

23. SCAVENGER HUNT

Students conduct a search for vocabulary items.

Sample Activity for Word by Word Picture Dictionary page 61:
Describing Clothing

Give students a list of certain items of clothing and have them walk around the school to find people who are wearing those items. For example:

Find someone who is wearing . . . .
1. a long-sleeved striped shirt
2. black sneakers
3. a solid color necktie
4. a checked shirt
   .
   .
   .

Students should write the person's name and a description of the article of clothing. The first person to successfully find all the clothing items is the winner.

24. TRUE OR FALSE?

Students answer *true or false* questions about the illustration in the Picture Dictionary.

Sample Activity for Word by Word Picture Dictionary page 16:
The Dining Room: A Place Setting

Make statements about the place setting on page 16 of the Picture Dictionary and have students decide whether the statements are true or false. If a statement is false, the student should correct it. For example:

The wine glass goes to the right of the water glass. [True]
The butter knife goes on the salad plate. [False. It goes on the bread-and-butter plate.]

VARIATION: Do the activity as a game with two competing teams.

DEFINITIONS

25. GUESS THE OBJECT

Students guess vocabulary items from their definitions.

Sample Activity for Word by Word Picture Dictionary page 87:
Office Equipment

Give the definition of an office equipment item and then ask, "What is it?"
For example:

> Teacher: You use it to do mathematic and scientific calculations.
> What is it?
> Student: A calculator.

This activity can also be done in pairs, in small groups, or as a game with competing teams.

26. CONCENTRATION

Students match vocabulary items with their definitions.

Sample Activity for Word by Word Picture Dictionary page 26:
The Apartment Building

a. Choose 9 apartment building words and for each make a matching set of cards—one with the word written on it and the other with the definition.

b. Shuffle the cards and place them face down in 3 rows of 6 each.

c. Divide the class into two teams. The object of the game is for students to find the matching cards. Both teams should be able to see the cards, since *concentrating* on their location is an important part of playing the game.

d. A student from Team 1 turns over two cards, and if they match that team gets a point and the student takes another turn. If they don't match, the student turns them face down and a member of Team 2 takes a turn.

e. The play continues until all the cards have been matched. The team with the most correct *matches* wins the game.

27. COOPERATIVE DEFINITIONS

Groups of students write definitions of vocabulary items for others to guess.

Sample Activity for Word by Word Picture Dictionary pages 80–84:
Occupations I/II

a. Divide the class into small groups of three or four. Give each group a letter designation (i.e. Group A, Group B . . .) and a piece of paper.

b. Ask each group to write definitions of five occupations.

c. When all the groups are ready, have them pass their papers with the definitions to the group on their right. Group A thus passes its definitions to Group B, who passes its definitions to Group C, etc.

d. Each group reads the definitions it has received, and on a separate piece of paper writes the group letter designation and what occupations they think are being defined.

e. Continue until each group has seen all the other groups' definitions.

f. Compare the results and see which group has the most correct guesses.

Note: To make sure there is a variety of occupations, you may want to assign five different occupations to each group.

28. CROSSWORDS

Students create crossword puzzles with vocabulary items.

Sample Activity for Word by Word Picture Dictionary page 90:
The Factory

a. Ask Student 1 to write a *factory word* in the middle of the board. For example:

> Student 1 writes WAREHOUSE on the board. (see below)

b. Then have Student 1 think of another factory word that can be linked vertically through a shared letter with the word on the board. The student gives a clue or definition of that word and tells the number of letters in the word and its first letter. For example:

> Student 1 says, "Something used to put out a fire. 16 letters. The first letter is F."

c. Student 2 comes to the board and writes the word so that it crosses the first word vertically, using the shared letter. For example:

> Student 2 writes FIRE EXTINGUISHER so that it crosses WAREHOUSE vertically at the shared letter R.

d. Student 2 then thinks of a word that can be linked horizontally through a shared letter with the second word and gives clues for that word. For example:

> Student 2 says, "A place where you can get a snack. 14 letters. The first letter is V."

e. Student 3 comes to the board and writes the word so that it crosses the second word horizontally, using the shared letter. For example:

> Student 3 writes VENDING MACHINE so that it crosses FIRE EXTINGUISHER horizontally at the shared letter G.

f. The activity continues, with students alternating vertical and horizontal linking words.

29. QUESTION THE ANSWER

Students create questions about vocabulary items.

Sample Activity for Word by Word Picture Dictionary page 22:
The Bathroom

   a. Write each word from page 22 of the Picture Dictionary on a separate card and put the cards face down on a table or desk in front of the room.

   b. Divide the class into two teams.

   c. A person from Team 1 comes to the front of the room, picks up a card, and silently reads the word. This is the answer.

   d. That person must then think of a question which that word could be the answer to. For example:

Card: toilet brush	Student: What do you use to clean the toilet?
Card: rubber mat	Student: What do you put in the bathtub so you won't fall?

If the team member *questions the answer* correctly, that team gets one point. If the person doesn't *question the answer* correctly, a member from the other team has a chance to answer it. The team with the most points wins the game.

30. TIC TAC DEFINITION

Students play a *tic tac toe* game with vocabulary items.

Sample Activity for Word by Word Picture Dictionary page 76:
The Library

a. Have each student make a grid with room for nine words and then fill in any nine vocabulary words they wish from page 76 of the Picture Dictionary. For example:

online catalog	call card	librarian
microfilm	reference section	media section
journal	checkout counter	information desk

b. Give definitions of library words and tell students to cross out any word they have written on their grids for which you have given the definition.

c. The first person to cross out three words in a straight line—either vertically, horizontally, or diagonally—wins the game.

31. WHAT'S THE QUESTION?

Students form questions based on definitions of vocabulary items.

Sample Activity for Word by Word Picture Dictionary page 58:
Sleepwear, Underwear, and Footwear

Describe an article of sleepwear, underwear, or footwear and have students respond by asking the question: "What's a/an _____?" or "What are _____s?"
For example:

> Teacher: It's worn over pajamas.
> Student: What's a bathrobe?

> Teacher: They're worn by both men and women under their clothing for warmth in colder climates.
> Student: What are longjohns?

This activity can be done as a game with competing teams. It can also be done by having teams come up with the descriptions which they then ask others.

CLUES

32. FINISH THE SENTENCE

Students complete sentences using vocabulary items.

Sample Activity for Word by Word Picture Dictionary page 10:
The Classroom

a. Divide the class into two teams.

b. Begin sentences and have students from each team take turns finishing them with appropriate words from page 10 of the Picture Dictionary. For example:

> Every student sits on a . . . . [chair].
> You tell the time by looking at the . . . . [clock].
> The person who helps the teacher is the . . . . [teacher's aide].
> We keep books in our classroom on the . . . . [bookshelf].
> You write on the board with . . . . [chalk].

c. The team with the most correctly completed sentences wins the game.

33. I'M THINKING OF A . . . THAT . . .

Students guess vocabulary items by listening to clues.

Sample Activity for Word by Word Picture Dictionary pages 46–47:
The Supermarket I

Make statements such as the following and have students guess the supermarket item you're thinking of. For example:

> A. I'm thinking of a diary product that starts with b.
> B. Butter.
>
> A. I'm thinking of a frozen food that people like for dessert.
> B. Ice cream.
>
> A. I'm thinking of a packaged good that many people have for breakfast.
> B. Cereal.

VARIATION: As a class, in pairs, in small groups, or as a game with competing teams, have individual students make the statements and others then guess the item.

34.   WHAT'S THE PLACE?

Students guess vocabulary items for places by listening to clues.

Sample Activity for Word by Word Picture Dictionary pages 34–37:
Places Around Town I/II

Describe a reason for going to places around town and have students guess which places you're talking about. For example:

You go there to see a play.	[theater]
You go there to see the animals.	[zoo]
You go there to get a haircut.	[barber shop]
You go there to buy tools.	[hardware store]
You go there when you're sick.	[clinic] [hospital]
You go there to look at paintings.	[museum]
You go there to exercise.	[health club]

VARIATION 1: Have students do this in pairs, taking turns describing and guessing.

VARIATION 2: Divide the class into two teams and do the activity as a game.

VARIATION 3: Write the reasons on cards. Have individual students or team members pick a card and name the place described.

35. WHO AM I?

Students guess vocabulary items for people by listening to clues.

Sample Activity for Word by Word Picture Dictionary page 72:
Medical and Dental Care

Describe the responsibilities of one of the health care professionals on page 72 of
the Picture Dictionary and have students guess who it is. For example:

> A. I tell you if you need glasses. Who am I?
> B. An optometrist.

> A. I come to your house quickly if you have an emergency. Who am I?
> B. An EMT.

VARIATION: You can also do this activity in pairs, in small groups, or as a game with
two competing teams.

36. WHISK!

Students replace the nonsense word *whisk* in sentences.

Sample Activity for Word by Word Picture Dictionary page 76:
The Library

Create sentences about the library, substituting the word *whisk* for the verb.
For example:

> "When I take a book from the library,
> I *whisk* it."   [borrow/check it out]

> "When I don't know where to find
> something, I *whisk*."   [ask for help/get help]

> "When I have to write a paper, I *whisk*   [do research]
> at the library."

VARIATION: Divide the class into small groups and have the groups create *"whisk"*
sentences for other students to figure out.

37. WHO IS SPEAKING?

Students match *quotes* to appropriate vocabulary items.

Sample Activity for Word by Word Picture Dictionary page 111:
Types of Entertainment

Create a television game show called *That's Entertainment!*

a. Divide the class into two teams.

b. Choose a student to be the host or hostess of the program.

c. Have the class design a set for the program and create commercials which they can present before, after, and during the breaks.

d. The object of the game is for contestants to identify the type of television program or movie based on a quote that the host or hostess reads to them. Let the class decide what the prizes are and what the rules of the game are.

POSSIBLE QUESTIONS:

"I cried when I saw that play."	[drama]
"That show really makes me laugh. I watch it every week."	[sitcom]
"My children love to watch those silly characters every Saturday morning."	[cartoon]
"I wish I could understand it without the subtitles."	[foreign film]
"Did you see the one where people from Pluto invaded New York City?"	[science fiction movie]
"I liked the part where they had to survive in the jungle with only a little food and no other supplies!"	[adventure movie]
"I don't like them. There's too much violence!"	[war movie]
"Most of them don't give an accurate picture of Native Americans."	[western]
"I can't believe the subjects they talk about!"	[talk show]
"I'm sure I'd be very nervous and not be able to answer any questions correctly!"	[game show]

38. IT'S SOMETHING THAT . . .

Groups of students guess vocabulary items based on clues given by team members.

Sample Activity for Word by Word Picture Dictionary page 15:
The Dining Room

a. Make up a set of cards with words from page 15 of the Picture Dictionary written on them.

b. Have students sit in groups of three or four, and give each group a set of the cards. Place the cards face down in the center of the group.

c. The first player takes the top card and, without showing it to the other players, gives a definition of the word. For example:

"It's something that's used for pouring drinks."

d. The first person to guess *pitcher* keeps the card. If nobody guesses correctly, the person who is holding the card keeps it and the next person takes a turn.

e. The player who has collected the most cards at the end of the game is the winner.

39.   HOT SPOT!

A student guesses vocabulary items based on clues given by team members.

Sample Activity for Word by Word Picture Dictionary page 88:
Office Furnishings

    a. Divide the class into two teams.

    b. Have one member from each team come to the front of the room and sit facing his or her teammates in the *hot spot.*

    c. Write one of the vocabulary words from page 88 of the Picture Dictionary on a piece of paper and show it to Team 1 without showing it to the person sitting in the front of the room.

    d. The team members then give clues to their teammate, who tries to guess the word.

    e. Repeat with Team 2.

    f. Continue until each team member has had a chance to sit in the *hot spot* and guess a word.

Scoring: Give each team a point for each clue given before the word is guessed. *Low score* wins the game.

40. WORD CLUES

Students give one-word clues for team members to guess the correct vocabulary item.

Sample Activity for Word by Word Picture Dictionary page 64:
Computers, Telephones, and Cameras

  a. Choose 10 computer, telephone, and camera items from page 64 of the Picture Dictionary and write each on a separate card.

  b. Divide the class into two teams.

  c. Have a member of each team come to the front of the room and sit facing his or her team.

  d. Show one of the vocabulary cards to the two players *without showing it to the rest of the class.*

  e. The two players take turns giving one-word clues to their teams so that they can guess the word. For example:

> The word is *fax machine.*

> Team 1 Player: "telephone"   [Team 1 guesses]
> Team 2 Player: "letter"   [Team 2 guesses]
> Team 1 Player: "fast"   [Team 1 guesses]

Tell each team to listen carefully to the opposing team's clues.

  f. Do the same for the remaining nine vocabulary words. The team that guesses the most words wins the game.

41. GENERAL TO SPECIFIC

Students guess vocabulary words by listening to clues that start out very general and gradually become more specific.

Sample Activity for Word by Word Picture Dictionary page 54:
Fast Foods and Sandwiches

a. Divide the class into two teams.

b. Make up clues that describe a fast food item. The clues should begin with general statements and become more specific. For example:

> Clue 1: I'm small.
> Clue 2: People eat me warm or cold.
> Clue 3: People usually cut me in half.
> Clue 4: I come in several varieties.
> Clue 5: People usually eat me for breakfast.
> Clue 6: I am round.
> Clue 7: I have a hole in the middle.
> Clue 8: People like to eat me with cream cheese.

> [Answer: a bagel]

c. Give a clue to Team 1. The students on that team have one chance to guess the word. If they don't guess correctly, ask Team 2. The play goes back and forth between the teams, with each team getting one more clue and one more chance to guess each time. The first team to guess the word wins a point.

d. Continue the game with more words and more clues. The team with the most points wins the game.

VARIATION:

a. Divide the class into several teams who write the clues themselves.

b. The teams take turns giving their clues to other teams, one at a time.

c. After each clue, students have a chance to guess what the word is. The team that guesses correctly wins a point. The team with the most points wins the game.

ASKING QUESTIONS

42. ASK ME A QUESTION!

Students ask each other questions to guess the meanings of vocabulary words.

Sample Activity for Word by Word Picture Dictionary pages 68–69:
The Body

a. Give each student a card with a word from the vocabulary list written on it.

b. Without showing the items on their cards, have students walk around and try to guess each other's words by asking yes/no questions. For example:

Is it part of your leg?	No.
Is it part of your hand?	No.
Is it part of your head?	Yes.
Is it your nose?	No.
Is it smaller than your nose?	No.
Is it your ear?	Yes.

VARIATION: Do the activity as a game by dividing the class into two teams. One person comes to the front of the room, thinks of a part of the body, and the two teams compete against each other, trying to guess the item by asking yes/no questions.

43.   WHAT AM I?

Students *become* the vocabulary items and try to guess each others' identities.

Sample Activity for Word by Word Picture Dictionary page 44:
Fruits

a. Write the name of a fruit on a card.

b. Pin a card on each person's back so the person doesn't see what fruit he or she *is*.

c. The person must discover his or her fruit by asking yes/no questions. For example:

> Am I round?
> Am I red?
> Do I have seeds?

This can be done as a class, in pairs, or in small groups. The person who guesses his or her fruit by asking the least number of questions *wins*.

44.   I'M THINKING OF SOMETHING

Groups try to guess a student's word by asking yes/no questions.

Sample Activity for Word by Word Picture Dictionary page 56:
Colors

a. Have students sit in groups of three or four.

b. One student in each group begins by thinking of an object and saying:

> "I'm thinking of something (color)."

c. The other students in the group then try to guess the object by asking yes/no questions. For example:

> [Thinking of a stop sign]
>
> Student 1: I'm thinking of something red.
> Student 2: Is it in this classroom?
> Student 1: No.
> Student 3: Is it found around the house?
> Student 1: No.
> Student 4: Is it found outside?
> Student 1: Yes.
>   etc.

45. GOT IT!

> **Group members rotate around the room asking yes/no questions to guess vocabulary words.**

Sample Activity for Word by Word Picture Dictionary page 20:
The Baby's Room

a. Divide the class into groups of four or five.

b. Have each group think of a word from the vocabulary list on page 20 of the Picture Dictionary that they want to make the other students guess.

c. When all the groups are ready, one member of each group goes and sits with the next group on the right.

d. The group members ask the visiting representative yes/no questions about the word until they guess it. For example:

> Is it a toy?
> Is it a piece of furniture?
> Does it have wheels?

e. When they guess the word, they call out "Got it!" That group gets a point for guessing correctly.

f. The representatives stay with the new group, another word is selected, a new representative is chosen, and the play continues as above.

46. MYSTERY WORD

> **A student guesses the class's word by asking yes/no questions.**

Sample Activity for Word by Word Picture Dictionary page 77:
The School

Ask one student to leave the room. Have the class choose a vocabulary word from page 77 of the Picture Dictionary. Ask the student to come back into the room and ask yes/no questions in order to guess the *mystery word* the class is thinking of. For example:

> Is it a person?
> Is it a place?
> Do people go there when they aren't feeling well?
> Do they eat there?

47. GUESS WHAT I'M THINKING OF!

The whole class tries to guess a student's word by asking yes/no questions.

Sample Activity for Word by Word Picture Dictionary page 57:
Clothing

a. Tell each student to think of an item of clothing.

b. Have a student come to the front of the room and say, "I'm thinking of an item of clothing."

c. The other students in the class try to guess the article of clothing by asking yes/no questions. For example:

> Is someone wearing it in this room?
> Is it short-sleeved?
> Is a female wearing it?
> Is it blue?

48. WHISK!

The whole class tries to guess a student's verb by asking questions with *whisk* instead of the verb.

Sample Activity for Word by Word Picture Dictionary page 9:
Everyday Activities II

a. A student chooses an everyday activity and sits facing the class.

b. The other students try to guess the activity by asking yes/no questions. In asking the questions, they should substitute the word *whisk* for the activity. For example:

> "Do you *whisk* every day?"
> "Do you *whisk* in the kitchen?"
> "Do you *whisk* for enjoyment?"
> "Is *whisking* a household chore?"

CATEGORIES

49. MOVABLE CATEGORIES

Students group themselves by category.

Sample Activity for Word by Word Picture Dictionary page 101:
The Beach

a. Give each student a card with a beach item written on it.

b. Call out one of the following categories:

Things to use in the sand.   Things to lie or sit on.
Things to use in the water.   Words which describe people.
Things for protection from the sun.   Activities you do at the beach.
Things to put on.   Things you carry to the beach.

c. All the students whose beach items are appropriate for that category go to the right side of the room. All other students go to the left side.

d. Those who are in the *right group* call out their words for the class to verify.

e. Continue with other categories.

For more advanced students, don't give any categories and have students group themselves any way they wish. Once groups are formed, they can either identify their categories or have students try to guess the category based on the beach words that are in each group.

50. DICTATION CATEGORIES

Students do a dictation using categorization.

Sample Activity for Word by Word Picture Dictionary page 101:
The Beach

a. Have students make four columns on a piece of paper.

b. Dictate any four of the categories in Activity 49 above and have students write each at the top of one of the columns.

c. Dictate beach items and have students write them in the appropriate column.

d. As a class, in pairs, or in small groups, have students check their work.

51. STAND UP CATEGORIES

Students stand up according to word categories.

Sample Activity for Word by Word Picture Dictionary page 62:
The Department Store

STAND UP FOR HOUSEWARES

a. Say the name of a department or section in a department store.

b. Tell students you're going to say four words. If they hear a word that is associated with that department or section, they should stand up. If they hear a word that is not associated with that department, they should sit down. For example:

Home Furnishings:	sofa	(stand up)
	coffee table	(remain standing)
	toaster	(sit down)
	blouse	(remain sitting)
Gift Wrap Counter:	paper towel	(remain sitting)
	ribbon	(stand up)
	calculator	(sit down)
	bow	(stand up)

35

52.   CATEGORY GAME

> **Students guess vocabulary items through a combination of clues and categories.**

Sample Activity for Word by Word Picture Dictionary page 56:
Colors

   a. Prepare index cards similar to the following:

Things that are green. grass broccoli lettuce	Things that are red. a stop sign a tomato spaghetti sauce
Things that are white. snow vanilla ice cream ceiling paint	Things that are blue. jeans the sky the ocean

You will need two of each index card you prepare.

   b. Divide the class into two teams.

   c. Ask one player from each team to come to the front of the room and sit facing his or her team.

   d. Give copies of the same card to each of the two players in the front. (Make sure these players understand all the words on the cards.)

   e. The first player announces the category: "Things that are green." That person then gives a clue for the first word. For example:

   > "It grows on the ground in front of houses and in parks."

   f. That person's teammates have one try to guess the answer. If they're correct they get a point and the team member gives a clue for the second word. If they don't guess the first word, the play goes to the other team, and they have a chance to guess the word based on the clue they've just heard.

   g. Continue the game with other color category cards. The team with the most points wins the game.

ASSOCIATIONS

53. GROUP ASSOCIATIONS

Groups of students brainstorm words associated with vocabulary items.

Sample Activity for Word by Word Picture Dictionary page 73:
Medical Treatment and the Hospital

a. Divide the class into small groups.

b. Call out a word from page 73 of the Picture Dictionary and have the groups write down as many associations as they can think of. For example:

        stitches: (cut/surgery/doctor/pain)
        cast: (broken leg/crutches/accident)

c. Have the groups call out their words and make a common list on the board.

d. Tell students they can question a word, in which case the student who suggested it must explain the reason for that association.

54. SECRET WORD ASSOCIATIONS

Students give words associated with a vocabulary item without naming the item.

Sample Activity for Word by Word Picture Dictionary pages 102–103:
Individual Sports and Recreation

In pairs or small groups, have students choose a *secret word* from the vocabulary list on pages 102–103 of the Picture Dictionary, brainstorm several associations, tell the associated words to the class, and see if students can guess the secret word.

55. WHAT CAN YOU DO IN . . . ?

Students brainstorm activities associated with vocabulary topics.

Sample Activity for Word by Word Picture Dictionary page 67:
The Bank

Have pairs or groups of students make a list of all the things you can do at a bank. For example:

cash a check	get travelers checks	apply for a loan
make a deposit	use an ATM card	put things in a safe deposit box

56. ASSOCIATION GAME

Students play a game based on associations.

Sample Activity for Word by Word Picture Dictionary page 62:
The Department Store

VARIATION 1:

a. Divide the class into several teams.

b. Call out the name of a department in a department store and have students in each group work together to see how many words they can associate with that department. For example:

Jewelry Department	(watch/rings/earrings/necklaces/ chains/lockets/pins/pearls)
Electronics Department:	(radios/TVs/CD players/tape recorders/ speakers/calculators)

The team with the most items wins.

VARIATION 2:

a. Divide the class into several teams.

b. Have each team decide on a department in a department store and some items that are purchased in that department. For example:

Women's Clothing Department: (shirts/dresses/coats/belts)

c. Each team reads its list *without telling the department,* and others guess what the department is.

The team with the most correct answers wins.

VARIATION 3:

a. Prepare index cards similar to the following:

Jewelry	Housewares
bracelet	frying pan
earrings	glasses
watch	coffee pot

You will need two of each index card you prepare.

b. Divide the class into two teams.

c. Ask one player from each team to come to the front of the room and sit facing his or her team.

d. Give copies of the same card to each of the two players in the front. (Make sure these players understand all the words on the cards.)

e. The first player announces the category: *Jewelry.* That person then gives a clue for the first word. For example:

> "You wear it around your wrist."

f. That person's teammates have one try to guess the answer. If they're correct, they get a point and the team member gives a clue for the second word. If they don't guess the first word, the play goes to the other team, and they have a chance to guess the word based on the clue they've just heard.

g. Continue the game with other departments. The team with the most points wins the game.

CONNECTIONS

57. CONNECTIONS

Students think of connections between two vocabulary items.

Sample Activity for Word by Word Picture Dictionary page 19:
Kitchenware

a. Write the words from page 19 of the Picture Dictionary on separate cards and put the cards in two piles on a table or desk in front of the room.

b. Have students pick one card from each pile and try to make a *connection* between the two items. The *connection* may be a similarity, a difference, or some relationship between the two. For example:

cake pan —— pie plate	Both are used for baking.
can opener —— saucepan	A can opener opens the soup which you heat in a saucepan.

VARIATION: The above activity can be done as a game with two competing teams.

58. OPPOSITES

Students give the opposites of vocabulary items.

Sample Activity for Word by Word Picture Dictionary pages 40–41:
Describing People and Things

Divide the class into two teams. Call out an adjective and have students raise their hands and tell you the opposite adjective. The team with the most correct answers wins.

VARIATION: Write the adjectives on flashcards. Students take turns picking the cards and giving the opposite adjective.

59. THINGS IN COMMON

Students brainstorm similarities between vocabulary items.

Sample Activity for Word by Word Picture Dictionary pages 80–84:
Occupations I/II

a. Divide the class into several teams.

b. Tell each team to think of two occupations that have some things in common and write down what those similarities are. For example:

> *barber / assembler*
> Both use their hands.
> Both work indoors.
> Both stand while they work.

> *bus driver / delivery person*
> Both use vehicles.
> Both go to different places around town.
> Both are used for transporting.

c. Each team reads the similarities *without naming the occupations,* and the other teams try to guess what the two occupations are. The team that guesses the most occupations wins the game.

60.   SAME AND DIFFERENT

Students brainstorm similarities and differences between vocabulary items.

Sample Activity for Word by Word Picture Dictionary page 89:
Office Supplies

a. Divide the class into small groups.

b. Write pairs of vocabulary words from page 89 of the Picture Dictionary on the board. For example:

envelope - mailer

c. Have the groups think of similarities and differences between each pair. For example:

Both are used to mail things.
Both take stamps.

An envelope is smaller than a mailer.
A mailer is thicker than an envelope.

61.   WHAT'S THE OBJECT?

Students brainstorm direct objects of *verb* vocabulary items.

Sample Activity for Word by Word Picture Dictionary page 11:
Classroom Actions

Call out a verb from the vocabulary list and have students add an appropriate direct object. For example:

close:	the book
raise:	your hand
answer:	the questions

VARIATION: Do the activity as a game with two competing teams.

DIALOGS

62. CONVERSATION FRAMEWORKS

Students use a dialog framework for vocabulary practice.

Sample Activity for Word by Word Picture Dictionary pages 42–43:
Describing Physical States and Emotions

WHY DO THEY FEEL THAT WAY?

a. Write the following on the board:

> A. How does he/she feel?
> B. He's/She's _____.
> A. Why?
> B. . . . .

b. Based on this conversational framework, have students give reasons for the way people are feeling in illustrations 1–32 on pages 42–43 of the Picture Dictionary. For example:

[3] A. How does she feel?
    B. She's exhausted.
    A. Why?
    B. She just ran five miles.

[15] A. How does he feel?
     B. He's disappointed.
     A. Why?
     B. Because he didn't win first prize.

63. BLEEP!

Students create dialogs containing *hidden* vocabulary words.

Sample Activity for Word by Word Picture Dictionary page 111:
Types of Entertainment

a. Write the numbered vocabulary words from page 111 of the Picture Dictionary on cards, mix up the cards, and put them face down in a pile on a table or desk in front of the room.

b. Divide the class into pairs.

c. Have each pair come to the front of the room, pick 2 cards from the pile, and create a conversation in which they use those two words.

d. Call on the pairs to present their conversations to the class. However, instead of saying the 2 words when they come up in the conversation, they say *bleep* instead!

e. Other students then try to guess the *bleeped* words and where the conversation is taking place.

64. MATCH GAME

Students match lines of dialog containing key vocabulary items.

Sample Activity for Word by Word Picture Dictionary page 27:
Housing Utilities, Services, and Repairs

a. Write the following problem situations and responses on separate cards.

b. Distribute the cards randomly to students in the class.

c. Have students memorize their lines and leave the cards on their desks.

d. Students should then walk around saying their lines until they find their *match*.

e. When all the pairs have been matched, have them say their lines for the whole class.

f. More advanced students can expand the lines into short dialogs which they perform for the class.

The stove is broken!	I can help you! I'm an appliance repair person!
The picture on my TV is very *fuzzy*!	I'll fix it! I'm a TV repair person!
Our front door is broken and we can't close it!	That's easy. I'm an excellent carpenter!
I'm so upset! I can't find my house keys!	Don't worry! I'm a locksmith!
I'd like to plant some bushes in front of my house.	I'll do it! I'm an experienced gardener!
My toilet won't flush!	I'll fix it! I'm a plumber!
My fireplace isn't working very well!	No problem! I'm a chimney sweep!
The light in my front hall is broken and I'm having trouble fixing it!	I can repair it! I'm an electrician!
We've got mice in our attic!	I'll take care of the problem. I'm an exterminator!

65. MYSTERY WORD CONVERSATIONS

Students create conversations about vocabulary items and others guess what the items are.

Sample Activity for Word by Word Picture Dictionary page 109:
Handicrafts, Hobbies, and Games

Divide the class into small groups. Have each group choose one of the handicrafts, hobbies, or games on page 109 of the Picture Dictionary and create a conversation that is about the chosen activity but never names that activity. The rest of the class tries to guess what the *mystery handicraft, hobby* or *game* is.

66. ROLE PLAYS

Students create role plays based on key vocabulary items.

Sample Activity for Word by Word Picture Dictionary page 99:
Outdoor Recreation

a. Give pairs of students a piece of paper and ask them to write two vocabulary words from page 99 of the Picture Dictionary.

b. Collect the papers and distribute them randomly to other pairs.

c. Each pair then creates a dialog using the words.

d. Have the pairs present their dialogs to the class.

DISCUSSION

67. CLASS DISCUSSION

The class has a discussion about the vocabulary topic.

Sample Activity for Word by Word Picture Dictionary pages 42–43:
Describing Physical States and Emotions

BODY LANGUAGE

a. Discuss with students the fact that we show how we feel not just by words but by our *body language*—our gestures, posture, and facial expressions.

b. Both you and students should demonstrate *non-verbally* emotions from the vocabulary list. Discuss cultural differences and similarities as the emotions are demonstrated.

VARIATION: Both you and students demonstrate body language and have others guess what the physical state or emotion is.

68. DAFFY DEBATE!

Students debate the *merits* of different vocabulary items.

Sample Activity for Word by Word Picture Dictionary page 24:
Household Cleaning and Laundry

a. Write each of the household cleaning and laundry items from page 24 of the Picture Dictionary on a separate card and put the cards face down on a table or desk in front of the room.

b. Two students come to the front of the room and each take a card.

c. The two must then have a one-minute *debate* on which item is more important for household cleaning.

d. After the debate, have the class vote on which person's reasons were more convincing.

e. Continue with other students and other *daffy debates.*

69. PAIR INTERVIEWS

Pairs of students discuss the topic vocabulary.

Sample Activity for Word by Word Picture Dictionary pages 78–79:
School Subjects and Extracurricular Activities

Divide the class into pairs. Have students interview each other about the classes they took or are taking in school. Have the pairs then report back to the class about their interviews. Sample interview questions:

> What is/was your favorite course? Why?
> What is/was your least favorite course? Why?
> What is/was your easiest course? Why?
> What is/was your most difficult course? Why?
> What is/was your most unusual course? Why?

70. PROBLEM SOLVING

Students offer suggestions involving the vocabulary items.

Sample Activity for Word by Word Picture Dictionary page 59:
Exercise Clothing and Outerwear

WHAT SHOULD I WEAR?

Tell some things you're going to do and have students suggest different items on page 59 of the Picture Dictionary to wear ("You should wear _____ " or "I think you should wear _____ ."). For example:

> "I'm going running. What should I wear?"
> "I'm going to aerobics class. What should I wear?"
> "I'm going for a bike ride. What should I wear?"
> "I'm going to the office and it's chilly. What should I wear?"
> "I'm going to a football game and it's very cold today. What should I wear?"

VARIATION: You can do this activity in pairs. One student tells his or her plans, and the other suggests what to wear.

71. TALK!

Sample Activity for Word by Word Picture Dictionary pages 68–69:
The Body

Give each student a card with the name of a part of the body written on it. Have students think about their word for a few minutes. Call on individual students to speak for one minute about their word. Encourage students to be as inventive as they wish in their presentations.

RESEARCH

72. FIELD TRIPS

Students visit a *real world* setting containing the topic vocabulary.

Sample Activity for Word by Word Picture Dictionary page 86:
The Office

Have students visit an office and write down all the vocabulary items they see as well as other words for office items. Have students report back to the class and talk about the new words.

73. INFORMATION SEARCH

Students do research on issues related to the topic vocabulary.

Sample Activity for Word by Word Picture Dictionary page 66:
Money

a. Ask students what money denominations they know from different countries around the world. Write the names on the board.

b. If students are interested, have them look up money denominations in other countries they would like to know about.

c. Have students call or visit a bank and find out what the current exchange rates are.

EXTENSIONS

74. IDIOMS

Students match idiomatic expressions with their definitions.

Sample Activity for Word by Word Picture Dictionary pages 48–49:
The Supermarket II

Divide the class into small groups or two teams. See if students can figure out what food item is part of the following idioms. The group with the most correct answers wins the competition.

1. "To bring home the _____" means to earn money for household expenses.

2. "To cry over spilled _____" means to get upset about something you can't do anything about.

3. When we think something is ridiculous or when we don't believe something, we say, "_____!"

4. "It's not my cup of _____" means I don't like it or it's not appropriate for me.

5. "To _____ someone up" means to flatter someone.

6. "To _____ someone on" means to tease someone.

7. "To lay an _____" means to fail at something or make a bad mistake.

8. A good person is sometimes called "a good _____."

9. If someone is "the _____ of the earth," that person is a good person that everyone can depend on.

10. "To take something with a grain of _____" means not to believe everything someone says.

11. "Let's talk _____!" means that we want to talk seriously about something.

12. "To _____ out" means to decide not to do something that frightens you.

13. "It's my _____ and _____", means it supplies me with the money I need to live.

14. We say, "_____'s on!" when dinner is ready.

15. "A hot _____" is a controversial topic you want to avoid discussing.

75. INVENTIONS

Students *invent* vocabulary items.

Sample Activity for Word by Word Picture Dictionary page 29:
Gardening Tools and Home Supplies

Individually, in pairs, or in small groups have students *invent* a gardening tool or home supply item. Have them draw a picture of the object, name it, and describe what it's used for. You may wish to have the class vote for the most original and most clever invention.

76. STORYTELLING

Students tell stories that include key vocabulary items.

Sample Activity for Word by Word Picture Dictionary page 100:
The Park and Playground

As a class, in pairs, or in small groups, have students create a story about the scene depicted on page 100 of the Picture Dictionary. Have them describe the scene and tell about the people and what they're doing.

VARIATION: Have students choose one of the people in the scene and tell a story about that person.

77. CHAIN STORY

Students create chain stories that incorporate vocabulary items.

Sample Activity for Word by Word Picture Dictionary page 95:
Public Transportation

a. Begin a story with an opener such as the following:

> "You won't believe what happened to me yesterday when I tried to take the train to New York!"

b. Have each student in turn add to the story. Encourage students to be as creative as they wish.

INDEX